EMMANUEL JOSEPH

The Decentralized Dream, Billionaires, Innovation, and the Quest for Sustainable Global Power

Copyright © 2025 by Emmanuel Joseph

All rights reserved. No part of this publication may be reproduced, stored or transmitted in any form or by any means, electronic, mechanical, photocopying, recording, scanning, or otherwise without written permission from the publisher. It is illegal to copy this book, post it to a website, or distribute it by any other means without permission.

First edition

This book was professionally typeset on Reedsy.
Find out more at reedsy.com

Contents

1. Chapter 1: The Dawn of Decentralization — 1
2. Chapter 2: The Billionaires' Playground — 3
3. Chapter 3: Innovators at the Helm — 5
4. Chapter 4: Sustainable Solutions — 7
5. Chapter 5: Revolutionizing Finance — 9
6. Chapter 6: Healthcare Reimagined — 11
7. Chapter 7: Education for All — 13
8. Chapter 8: Governance and Democracy — 15
9. Chapter 9: Energy for the Future — 17
10. Chapter 10: The Rise of the Digital Nomad — 19
11. Chapter 11: The Social Impact of Decentralization — 21
12. Chapter 12: The Environmental Promise — 23
13. Chapter 13: Building Resilient Communities — 25
14. Chapter 14: The Role of Technology — 27
15. Chapter 15: The Ethics of Decentralization — 29
16. Chapter 16: The Quest for Sustainable Power — 31
17. Chapter 17: The Future of Decentralization — 33

1

Chapter 1: The Dawn of Decentralization

In the early 21st century, the concept of decentralization began to revolutionize industries worldwide. Rooted in the ideals of democratizing power and resources, decentralization offered a promising future where control was distributed rather than concentrated. This chapter delves into the historical context of decentralization, tracing its origins back to the rise of the internet and blockchain technology. It explores how these technological advancements laid the groundwork for a more equitable distribution of power and wealth, challenging traditional hierarchies and paving the way for innovative solutions to global problems.

As societies grappled with the implications of decentralized systems, early adopters recognized the potential for these technologies to disrupt existing power structures. Visionaries and entrepreneurs saw opportunities to create more transparent, efficient, and resilient systems, driving a wave of innovation that would reshape industries from finance to healthcare. This chapter examines the pioneers of decentralization and their contributions to the movement, highlighting the breakthroughs that sparked a global shift towards a more decentralized future.

The rise of decentralized technologies also brought new challenges and ethical considerations. As power shifted away from centralized institutions, questions emerged about accountability, security, and the potential for misuse. This chapter explores the complex landscape of decentralization, examining the risks and rewards of a more distributed system. It delves into the debates surrounding regulation and governance, highlighting the need for a balanced approach that safeguards innovation while protecting the public interest.

In the face of these challenges, the decentralized dream continued to gain momentum, driven by a growing community of advocates and innovators. This chapter concludes by reflecting on the transformative potential of decentralization and the collective efforts to build a more inclusive and sustainable global future. It sets the stage for the journey ahead, as we explore the impact of decentralization on billionaires, innovation, and the quest for sustainable global power.

2

Chapter 2: The Billionaires' Playground

As decentralization gained traction, it inevitably attracted the attention of the world's wealthiest individuals. Billionaires, with their vast resources and influence, began to see the potential for leveraging decentralized technologies to expand their empires and drive global change. This chapter delves into the motivations and ambitions of these powerful figures, exploring how they embraced decentralization as a means to achieve their goals.

The billionaires' playground was a landscape of immense opportunities and fierce competition. With the rise of cryptocurrencies and blockchain technology, new avenues for wealth creation emerged, allowing these titans of industry to further consolidate their power. This chapter examines the key players in this arena, highlighting their strategies and investments in decentralized technologies. It also explores the ways in which these billionaires used their influence to shape the development of the decentralized movement, for better or for worse.

However, the concentration of wealth and power among a select few raised important questions about the true potential of decentralization. Critics argued that the involvement of billionaires could undermine the movement's core principles, perpetuating existing inequalities rather than addressing them. This chapter explores these tensions, examining the complex relationship between wealth, power, and decentralization. It delves into the ethical dilemmas and trade-offs faced by those who sought to balance profit with purpose.

Despite these challenges, the billionaires' playground also saw remarkable innovations and breakthroughs. This chapter highlights the successes and failures of these influential figures, showcasing the ways in which their investments and initiatives have shaped the trajectory of decentralization. It concludes by reflecting on the lessons learned from their experiences, setting the stage for a deeper exploration of the role of innovation in the quest for sustainable global power.

3

Chapter 3: Innovators at the Helm

The decentralized dream would not have been possible without the tireless efforts of innovators who pushed the boundaries of technology and imagination. This chapter celebrates the trailblazers who played a pivotal role in driving the decentralization movement forward. From visionary entrepreneurs to pioneering scientists, these individuals harnessed the power of decentralized technologies to create solutions that addressed pressing global challenges.

Innovation at the helm of decentralization was characterized by a relentless pursuit of progress and a willingness to challenge the status quo. This chapter profiles some of the most influential innovators in the field, exploring their journeys, motivations, and contributions to the movement. It delves into their groundbreaking projects and the impact they had on industries ranging from finance to healthcare, highlighting the transformative potential of decentralization.

At the heart of these innovations was a commitment to creating systems that were more transparent, efficient, and resilient. This chapter examines the core principles that guided these pioneers, including the importance of collaboration, open-source development, and user empowerment. It also explores the role of innovation hubs and communities in fostering the exchange of ideas and driving collective progress.

The journey of these innovators was not without its challenges. This chapter delves into the obstacles they faced, from regulatory hurdles to technological limitations. It highlights the resilience and perseverance that defined their efforts, showcasing how they overcame these barriers to realize their visions. It concludes by reflecting on the ongoing contributions of these trailblazers to the decentralization movement and their legacy in shaping a more sustainable global future.

4

Chapter 4: Sustainable Solutions

As the world grappled with the urgent need for sustainable development, decentralization emerged as a powerful tool for driving meaningful change. This chapter explores how decentralized technologies and approaches have been harnessed to create sustainable solutions across various sectors. From renewable energy to resource management, decentralization offered innovative ways to address environmental challenges and promote social equity.

The promise of sustainable solutions lay in the ability to distribute resources and decision-making power more equitably. This chapter examines the key areas where decentralization has made a significant impact, highlighting successful case studies and projects. It delves into the role of decentralized energy grids, peer-to-peer resource sharing, and community-driven initiatives in promoting sustainability and resilience.

At the core of these sustainable solutions was a commitment to empowering local communities and fostering collaboration. This chapter explores the ways in which decentralized approaches enabled greater participation and ownership, allowing individuals and communities to take charge of their own development. It also examines the role of technology in facilitating these efforts, from blockchain-based tracking systems to decentralized platforms for knowledge sharing.

The journey towards sustainable solutions was not without its challenges.

This chapter delves into the obstacles faced by those working to implement decentralized approaches, from regulatory barriers to technical complexities. It highlights the importance of adaptive strategies and continuous innovation in overcoming these challenges. It concludes by reflecting on the potential of decentralization to drive a more sustainable and inclusive global future, setting the stage for further exploration in the chapters to come.

5

Chapter 5: Revolutionizing Finance

Decentralization had a profound impact on the world of finance, giving rise to new paradigms and disrupting traditional banking systems. This chapter explores how decentralized finance (DeFi) revolutionized the way people managed, invested, and transferred money. By leveraging blockchain technology, DeFi platforms provided greater transparency, security, and accessibility, empowering individuals to take control of their financial futures.

At the heart of this revolution was the elimination of intermediaries, such as banks and financial institutions, which often acted as gatekeepers to financial services. This chapter examines the key innovations in DeFi, including smart contracts, decentralized exchanges, and peer-to-peer lending platforms. It delves into the benefits of these technologies, such as reduced transaction costs, increased speed, and enhanced security, highlighting the ways in which DeFi democratized access to financial services.

The rise of DeFi also brought new challenges and risks. This chapter explores the regulatory and security concerns associated with decentralized finance, including issues of fraud, hacking, and market volatility. It examines the efforts of industry leaders and policymakers to address these challenges, emphasizing the need for robust regulatory frameworks and innovative solutions to ensure the safety and stability of DeFi platforms.

Despite these obstacles, the impact of DeFi on the global financial system was undeniable. This chapter highlights the transformative potential of decentralized finance, showcasing successful case studies and projects that demonstrated the power of DeFi to create more inclusive and resilient financial systems. It concludes by reflecting on the future of finance in a decentralized world, setting the stage for further exploration of the intersection between innovation and sustainability.

6

Chapter 6: Healthcare Reimagined

The decentralized dream extended beyond finance, offering new possibilities for the healthcare industry. This chapter explores how decentralized technologies transformed healthcare delivery, enabling more personalized, efficient, and accessible care. From telemedicine to blockchain-based health records, decentralization offered innovative solutions to address the challenges of modern healthcare.

At the core of this transformation was the ability to empower patients with greater control over their health data and care decisions. This chapter examines the key innovations in decentralized healthcare, including patient-owned health records, decentralized clinical trials, and AI-driven diagnostics. It delves into the benefits of these technologies, such as improved data security, enhanced patient privacy, and increased access to care, highlighting the ways in which decentralization democratized healthcare.

However, the implementation of decentralized healthcare was not without its challenges. This chapter explores the regulatory, technical, and ethical considerations associated with decentralized health systems, including issues of data interoperability, patient consent, and equitable access. It examines the efforts of healthcare providers, technology developers, and policymakers to address these challenges, emphasizing the importance of collaboration and patient-centered design.

The impact of decentralized healthcare on patient outcomes and system efficiency was significant. This chapter highlights successful case studies and projects that demonstrated the power of decentralization to improve health outcomes, reduce costs, and enhance patient satisfaction. It concludes by reflecting on the future of healthcare in a decentralized world, setting the stage for further exploration of the potential of technology to drive sustainable global development.

7

Chapter 7: Education for All

Decentralization also had a profound impact on the education sector, offering new opportunities for learning and personal development. This chapter explores how decentralized technologies transformed education delivery, enabling more personalized, accessible, and inclusive learning experiences. From online learning platforms to blockchain-based credentialing, decentralization offered innovative solutions to address the challenges of modern education.

At the heart of this transformation was the ability to empower learners with greater control over their educational journeys. This chapter examines the key innovations in decentralized education, including personalized learning pathways, decentralized certification systems, and peer-to-peer knowledge sharing platforms. It delves into the benefits of these technologies, such as increased access to high-quality education, enhanced learner engagement, and improved skills recognition, highlighting the ways in which decentralization democratized education.

The implementation of decentralized education was not without its challenges. This chapter explores the regulatory, technical, and cultural considerations associated with decentralized learning systems, including issues of quality assurance, data privacy, and digital literacy. It examines the efforts of educators, technology developers, and policymakers to address these challenges, emphasizing the importance of learner-centered design and equitable access to educational opportunities.

The impact of decentralized education on learners and educational institutions was significant. This chapter highlights successful case studies and projects that demonstrated the power of decentralization to enhance learning outcomes, foster innovation, and promote lifelong learning. It concludes by reflecting on the future of education in a decentralized world, setting the stage for further exploration of the potential of technology to drive sustainable global development.

8

Chapter 8: Governance and Democracy

Decentralization also offered new possibilities for governance and democratic participation, enabling more transparent, accountable, and inclusive decision-making processes. This chapter explores how decentralized technologies transformed governance structures, empowering citizens with greater control over their political and civic lives. From blockchain-based voting systems to decentralized autonomous organizations (DAOs), decentralization offered innovative solutions to address the challenges of modern governance.

At the core of this transformation was the ability to distribute power more equitably and transparently. This chapter examines the key innovations in decentralized governance, including smart contracts for public administration, decentralized voting platforms, and community-driven policy development. It delves into the benefits of these technologies, such as enhanced transparency, reduced corruption, and increased citizen engagement, highlighting the ways in which decentralization democratized governance.

The implementation of decentralized governance systems was not without its challenges. This chapter explores the regulatory, technical, and ethical considerations associated with decentralized governance, including issues of data integrity, voter privacy, and equitable representation. It examines the efforts of policymakers, technology developers, and civic organizations to address these challenges, emphasizing the importance of participatory design and robust regulatory frameworks.

The impact of decentralized governance on political and civic life was significant. This chapter highlights successful case studies and projects that demonstrated the power of decentralization to enhance democratic participation, foster accountability, and promote social equity. It concludes by reflecting on the future of governance in a decentralized world, setting the stage for further exploration of the potential of technology to drive sustainable global development.

9

Chapter 9: Energy for the Future

Decentralization offered transformative possibilities for the energy sector, enabling more sustainable and resilient energy systems. This chapter explores how decentralized technologies have been harnessed to create innovative solutions for energy generation, distribution, and consumption. From renewable energy microgrids to peer-to-peer energy trading, decentralization has provided new ways to address the global energy crisis and promote environmental sustainability.

At the core of this transformation was the shift towards localized, community-driven energy systems. This chapter examines the key innovations in decentralized energy, including solar and wind energy microgrids, blockchain-based energy trading platforms, and energy storage solutions. It delves into the benefits of these technologies, such as increased energy efficiency, enhanced grid resilience, and reduced greenhouse gas emissions, highlighting the ways in which decentralization has democratized access to clean energy.

The implementation of decentralized energy systems was not without its challenges. This chapter explores the regulatory, technical, and economic considerations associated with decentralized energy, including issues of grid integration, energy pricing, and policy support. It examines the efforts of energy providers, technology developers, and policymakers to address these challenges, emphasizing the importance of collaboration and adaptive strategies.

The impact of decentralized energy on communities and the environment was significant. This chapter highlights successful case studies and projects that demonstrated the power of decentralization to enhance energy security, promote environmental sustainability, and empower local communities. It concludes by reflecting on the future of energy in a decentralized world, setting the stage for further exploration of the potential of technology to drive sustainable global development.

10

Chapter 10: The Rise of the Digital Nomad

The advent of decentralization brought about a cultural shift in the way people worked and lived. This chapter explores how decentralized technologies enabled the rise of the digital nomad lifestyle, allowing individuals to work remotely and live independently of traditional office environments. From remote work platforms to decentralized coworking spaces, decentralization provided new opportunities for flexibility, mobility, and work-life balance.

At the heart of this cultural shift was the ability to leverage technology to create more flexible and adaptable work environments. This chapter examines the key innovations in decentralized work, including remote collaboration tools, decentralized coworking platforms, and blockchain-based freelance marketplaces. It delves into the benefits of these technologies, such as increased productivity, enhanced work-life balance, and greater access to global job opportunities, highlighting the ways in which decentralization has transformed the world of work.

The rise of the digital nomad lifestyle also brought new challenges and considerations. This chapter explores the regulatory, logistical, and social implications of decentralized work, including issues of labor rights, taxation, and community building. It examines the efforts of employers, technology developers, and policymakers to address these challenges, emphasizing the importance of creating supportive ecosystems and policies for remote workers.

The impact of the digital nomad lifestyle on individuals and society was profound. This chapter highlights successful case studies and stories of digital nomads who have embraced decentralized work to achieve greater freedom and fulfillment. It concludes by reflecting on the future of work in a decentralized world, setting the stage for further exploration of the potential of technology to drive cultural and social change.

11

Chapter 11: The Social Impact of Decentralization

Decentralization had far-reaching implications for social structures and relationships, offering new possibilities for community building, social inclusion, and empowerment. This chapter explores how decentralized technologies have been harnessed to create positive social impact, addressing issues of inequality, access, and participation. From decentralized social networks to community-driven initiatives, decentralization provided new ways to foster social cohesion and resilience.

At the core of this social transformation was the ability to create more inclusive and participatory systems. This chapter examines the key innovations in decentralized social impact, including decentralized social media platforms, community-driven funding models, and blockchain-based identity solutions. It delves into the benefits of these technologies, such as enhanced privacy, increased social capital, and greater access to resources and opportunities, highlighting the ways in which decentralization has democratized social participation.

The implementation of decentralized social impact initiatives was not without its challenges. This chapter explores the regulatory, ethical, and cultural considerations associated with decentralized social systems, including issues of digital inclusion, data privacy, and cultural sensitivity. It examines the efforts of social innovators, technology developers, and policymakers to address these challenges, emphasizing the importance of community-centered design and inclusive practices.

The impact of decentralization on social structures and relationships was significant. This chapter highlights successful case studies and projects that demonstrated the power of decentralization to enhance social inclusion, promote community resilience, and empower marginalized groups. It concludes by reflecting on the future of social impact in a decentralized world, setting the stage for further exploration of the potential of technology to drive social and cultural change.

12

Chapter 12: The Environmental Promise

Decentralization also held great promise for addressing environmental challenges and promoting sustainable development. This chapter explores how decentralized technologies have been harnessed to create innovative solutions for environmental conservation, resource management, and climate action. From decentralized environmental monitoring to community-driven conservation efforts, decentralization offered new ways to address the global environmental crisis.

At the core of this promise was the ability to create more adaptive and resilient environmental systems. This chapter examines the key innovations in decentralized environmental solutions, including blockchain-based environmental tracking, decentralized resource management platforms, and community-driven conservation initiatives. It delves into the benefits of these technologies, such as enhanced data accuracy, increased stakeholder engagement, and improved resource efficiency, highlighting the ways in which decentralization has democratized environmental stewardship.

The implementation of decentralized environmental solutions was not without its challenges. This chapter explores the regulatory, technical, and social considerations associated with decentralized environmental systems, including issues of data interoperability, stakeholder coordination, and equitable access. It examines the efforts of environmental organizations, technology developers, and policymakers to address these challenges, emphasizing the importance of collaborative approaches and adaptive management.

The impact of decentralization on environmental conservation and resource management was significant. This chapter highlights successful case studies and projects that demonstrated the power of decentralization to enhance environmental outcomes, promote sustainable development, and empower local communities. It concludes by reflecting on the future of environmental stewardship in a decentralized world, setting the stage for further exploration of the potential of technology to drive sustainable global development.

13

Chapter 13: Building Resilient Communities

Decentralization empowered communities to become more self-reliant and resilient in the face of global challenges. This chapter explores how decentralized technologies have been harnessed to strengthen community resilience, enhance local economies, and promote social cohesion. From decentralized disaster response systems to community-driven economic development initiatives, decentralization offered new ways to build stronger, more adaptive communities.

At the core of this transformation was the ability to leverage local knowledge and resources to create tailored solutions that addressed the unique needs of each community. This chapter examines the key innovations in decentralized community resilience, including blockchain-based disaster response platforms, decentralized community currencies, and peer-to-peer support networks. It delves into the benefits of these technologies, such as increased community engagement, enhanced social capital, and improved resource allocation, highlighting the ways in which decentralization has democratized community development.

The implementation of decentralized community resilience initiatives was not without its challenges. This chapter explores the regulatory, technical, and social considerations associated with decentralized community systems, including issues of data privacy, stakeholder coordination, and equitable access. It examines the efforts of community leaders, technology developers, and policymakers to address these challenges, emphasizing the importance of community-centered design and inclusive practices.

The impact of decentralization on community resilience and local economies was significant. This chapter highlights successful case studies and projects that demonstrated the power of decentralization to enhance community resilience, promote economic development, and foster social cohesion. It concludes by reflecting on the future of community development in a decentralized world, setting the stage for further exploration of the potential of technology to drive social and economic change.

14

Chapter 14: The Role of Technology

Decentralization was driven by rapid advancements in technology, which enabled new ways of organizing and managing resources, information, and power. This chapter explores the role of technology in the decentralization movement, examining the key innovations and breakthroughs that have shaped its trajectory. From blockchain and artificial intelligence to the Internet of Things (IoT), technology provided the foundation for a more decentralized and interconnected world.

At the heart of this technological revolution was the ability to create more transparent, secure, and efficient systems. This chapter examines the key technologies that have driven decentralization, including distributed ledger technology, decentralized applications (dApps), and smart contracts. It delves into the benefits of these technologies, such as enhanced data security, increased automation, and improved interoperability, highlighting the ways in which technology has democratized access to information and resources.

The development and implementation of decentralized technologies were not without their challenges. This chapter explores the technical, regulatory, and ethical considerations associated with decentralized systems, including issues of scalability, data privacy, and algorithmic bias. It examines the efforts of technology developers, researchers, and policymakers to address these challenges, emphasizing the importance of collaboration and responsible innovation.

The impact of technology on the decentralization movement was profound. This chapter highlights successful case studies and projects that demonstrated the power of technology to drive decentralization and create more inclusive and resilient systems. It concludes by reflecting on the future of technology in a decentralized world, setting the stage for further exploration of the potential of innovation to drive sustainable global development.

15

Chapter 15: The Ethics of Decentralization

The decentralization movement raised important ethical questions about the distribution of power, resources, and decision-making authority. This chapter explores the ethical considerations associated with decentralization, examining the potential benefits and risks of creating more distributed systems. From issues of equity and fairness to questions of accountability and transparency, decentralization presented both opportunities and challenges for ethical governance.

At the core of these ethical considerations was the need to balance the benefits of decentralization with the potential for unintended consequences. This chapter examines the key ethical issues associated with decentralized systems, including issues of access and inclusion, data privacy, and social justice. It delves into the debates surrounding the ethical implications of decentralization, highlighting the ways in which different stakeholders have navigated these complex questions.

The ethical challenges of decentralization were not easily resolved, requiring ongoing dialogue and reflection. This chapter explores the efforts of ethicists, policymakers, and technology developers to address the ethical considerations of decentralization, emphasizing the importance of participatory governance and ethical design. It examines the role of ethical frameworks and guidelines in shaping the development and implementation of decentralized systems.

The impact of ethical considerations on the decentralization movement was significant. This chapter highlights successful case studies and projects that demonstrated the ways in which ethical principles have been integrated into decentralized systems, promoting greater transparency, accountability, and social justice. It concludes by reflecting on the future of ethics in a decentralized world, setting the stage for further exploration of the potential of ethical governance to drive sustainable global development.

16

Chapter 16: The Quest for Sustainable Power

The ultimate goal of the decentralization movement was to create more sustainable and equitable systems of power and resource distribution. This chapter explores the quest for sustainable power, examining the ways in which decentralized technologies have been harnessed to promote environmental sustainability, social equity, and economic resilience. From decentralized energy systems to community-driven development initiatives, decentralization offered new possibilities for creating a more sustainable and inclusive global future.

At the heart of this quest was the recognition that traditional systems of power and resource distribution were often inefficient, inequitable, and unsustainable. This chapter examines the key innovations in sustainable power, including decentralized renewable energy systems, blockchain-based supply chain management, and community-driven economic development initiatives. It delves into the benefits of these technologies, such as increased resource efficiency, enhanced social equity, and improved environmental outcomes, highlighting the ways in which decentralization has democratized access to power and resources.

The quest for sustainable power was not without its challenges. This chapter explores the regulatory, technical, and social considerations associated with decentralized systems of power and resource distribution, including issues of scalability, data privacy, and stakeholder coordination. It examines the efforts of technology developers, policymakers, and community leaders to address these challenges, emphasizing the importance of collaboration and adaptive strategies.

The impact of decentralized systems of power and resource distribution on global sustainability was significant. This chapter highlights successful case studies and projects that demonstrated the power of decentralization to promote sustainable development, enhance social equity, and empower local communities. It concludes by reflecting on the future of sustainable power in a decentralized world, setting the stage for the final chapter of the book.

17

Chapter 17: The Future of Decentralization

As we look to the future, the promise of decentralization remains as compelling as ever. This chapter explores the potential of decentralization to drive continued innovation, promote social equity, and create more sustainable and resilient systems. From emerging technologies to evolving social and economic dynamics, decentralization offers new possibilities for shaping a better global future.

At the heart of this vision for the future is the recognition that decentralization is an ongoing process, requiring continuous innovation, adaptation, and collaboration. This chapter examines the key trends and developments that will shape the future of decentralization, including advancements in technology, shifts in regulatory frameworks, and the growing importance of global collaboration. It delves into the potential benefits and challenges of these trends, highlighting the ways in which decentralization can create more inclusive and sustainable systems.

The future of decentralization also requires a commitment to ethical governance and responsible innovation. This chapter explores the importance of integrating ethical principles and inclusive practices into the development and implementation of decentralized systems. It examines the role of policymakers, technology developers, and global citizens in promoting ethical governance and ensuring that the benefits of decentralization are equitably distributed.

The impact of decentralization on the future of global development is profound. This chapter highlights successful case studies and visionary projects that demonstrate the potential of decentralization to drive positive change. It concludes by reflecting on the journey of the decentralization movement, celebrating its achievements, and envisioning a future where the dream of decentralization becomes a reality for all.

Book Description: "The Decentralized Dream: Billionaires, Innovation, and the Quest for Sustainable Global Power"

In an era defined by rapid technological advancements and shifting power dynamics, "The Decentralized Dream" explores the transformative potential of decentralization in reshaping our world. This compelling narrative takes readers on a journey through the key facets of decentralization, from its impact on billionaires and innovation to its promise of creating more sustainable and equitable global systems.

The book delves into the origins and evolution of decentralization, highlighting the pioneers and visionaries who have driven this movement forward. Through vivid storytelling and insightful analysis, it examines the ways in which decentralized technologies—such as blockchain, decentralized finance (DeFi), and peer-to-peer networks—are revolutionizing industries and challenging traditional power structures.

As the narrative unfolds, readers are introduced to the billionaires who have embraced decentralization, leveraging their wealth and influence to shape its trajectory. The book explores the ethical dilemmas and trade-offs faced by these powerful figures, as well as their successes and failures in navigating this complex landscape.

Beyond the realm of wealth and power, "The Decentralized Dream" also delves into the impact of decentralization on key sectors such as healthcare, education, energy, and governance. Through a series of compelling case studies and real-world examples, it demonstrates how decentralized technologies are driving meaningful change and promoting social equity, environmental sustainability, and community resilience.

CHAPTER 17: THE FUTURE OF DECENTRALIZATION

As readers journey through the chapters, they gain a deeper understanding of the ethical considerations, regulatory challenges, and technical innovations that shape the future of decentralization. The book concludes by envisioning a future where the decentralized dream becomes a reality, offering new possibilities for a more inclusive, transparent, and sustainable global society.

"The Decentralized Dream" is a thought-provoking exploration of the potential of decentralization to transform our world. It is a must-read for anyone interested in understanding the dynamics of power, innovation, and sustainability in the 21st century.

www.ingramcontent.com/pod-product-compliance
Ingram Content Group UK Ltd.
Pitfield, Milton Keynes, MK11 3LW, UK
UKHW031030120325
456161UK00006B/494